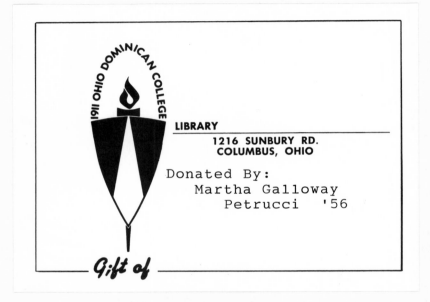

THE THANKSGIVING STORY

THE
THANKSGIVING STORY

by ALICE DALGLIESH

with illustrations by HELEN SEWELL

NEW YORK   CHARLES SCRIBNER'S SONS

AUTHOR'S NOTE

In writing the text and making the pictures for this book, Helen Sewell and I have kept them both very simple —so they tell the story of one family and of the changing seasons.

The Pilgrims and settlers were chiefly a group of country people— farmers, weavers, and other workmen. They wore the clothes of the time —perhaps less elaborate—and they wore colors. The wide, tall hats were expensive, so the men and boys had knitted and cloth caps for ordinary occasions.

The plan of the *Mayflower* (which is a plan of a typical ship of the period) and the map are by Rafael Palacios.

O-9.72 [RD]

SBN 684-12330-4

Copyright 1954 by ALICE DALGLIESH and HELEN SEWELL

PRINTED IN THE UNITED STATES OF AMERICA

THE THANKSGIVING STORY

THIS IS THE STORY
OF THE FIRST THANKSGIVING IN AMERICA.
IT HAPPENED MORE THAN THREE HUNDRED YEARS AGO.

TWO SHIPS
AND A BIG ADVENTURE

It was a summer day in England. Giles, Constance, and Damaris Hopkins were on their way to America.

As they waited, with their father and mother, on the ship, they could see a great deal going on around them.

They were in the harbor of the town of Southampton. Many ships were in the harbor. Two of them were taking on food and water and all the things needed by people going to a new country.

The larger ship was the *Mayflower*. The smaller one was the *Speedwell*.

Men, women, and children were on the ships, with their bundles and their boxes. To the children, it was a great adventure. Anything might happen on a ship.

Something special would happen to the Hopkins family on the long voyage.

The passengers on the *Mayflower* and the *Speedwell* were of many different kinds.

All of them were settlers, going to settle or make homes in a new land.

Some of them were the people that we call Pilgrims. A pilgrim is a person who travels to a far-off place because of his religion. In England at that time everyone had to go to the same church. The Pilgrims wanted to be free to have their own church, to worship God in their own way. So they had left England and gone to live in Holland. Now they had come back from Holland to sail for America.

Some of the people on the ships were servants and a few were hired workmen. A carpenter, like John Alden, would be useful in the new land.

Some people were going just for adventure. Others were going because they thought England was crowded. There would be more room to farm in America.

Between the decks there was a room or space for the passengers. The sailors called this 'tween decks.

In the lower part or hold of the ship were barrels of water and of food.

There were seeds to plant and tools for planting them. There were saws, axes and hammers for building houses.

Some of the barrels held things for trading with Indians. There was bright-colored cloth. There were beads and knives and little mirrors – all things that they had heard the Indians liked to have.

The Mayflower

Upper Deck
'tween Decks
Cabin
Gun
Room
HOLD

Now the time had come for the ships to start on the great adventure. The children would have liked to be on deck, to see the land as they sailed away from it.

But the sailors were very busy. The captain gave orders for the passengers to stay down below until the ships were out of the harbor. Only the sailors could be on deck while the sails were being set.

How crowded it was below decks! Passengers had small mattresses on the floor, each close to the next one. There were some wooden bunks or ship's beds. A few people had cabins.

In their cabin, Giles, Constance, and Damaris listened. They heard the rattle of the chain as the anchor was raised. They heard the sailors singing. They heard the creak, creak of the ropes as the sailors worked with the sails. The big white sails would fill with wind and move the ship across the ocean.

"May we go on deck now?"

"Not until the sails are set."

More strange noises and more time to wait. Then the ships were out in the ocean.

Soon the captain of the *Speedwell* put up signal flags. These flags told the other ship that the *Speedwell* was in trouble. She was leaking and could not go on. Perhaps her captain was afraid to take such a small ship on such a long voyage.

Both ships sailed back to land. Some of the passengers from the *Speedwell* stayed in England. Some of them went on the *Mayflower*. That made the *Mayflower* more crowded than ever. There were a hundred and two passengers on that small ship. Many of them were children.

A SHIP SAILS ALONE

This time the *Mayflower* sailed from Plymouth.

Out into the wide ocean went the little ship. Now she was all alone. Soon even the seagulls that followed her had flown back to shore.

Many people were seasick. Others were sick because they did not have fresh fruit and vegetables to eat.

Most days they ate hard biscuits and salted or dried meat. A few times a week they could make a charcoal fire on sand placed in an iron box and sit around it to get warm. Then they cooked a big pot of porridge or soup or stew. Nothing felt so good as that warm food in the stomach.

Warm days, sunny days, gray days, rainy days.

Then came a big storm. How the waves beat against the ship! Everyone was afraid. Perhaps they would have to go back to England.

After the storm, the sea grew calmer, and the Pilgrims gave thanks to God. A baby was born to the Hopkins family. A baby brother for Giles, Constance, and Damaris!

What was the new baby to be called?

Some of the children on the ship had names like Love, Resolved, Humility, and Remember.

There seemed to be only one name for a child born on the ocean.

And so the Hopkins baby was called OCEANUS.

The *Mayflower* sailed on and on. The days and nights grew colder. There was plenty of time to talk about Virginia, the part of America where they were going. It would be warm there, with sunshine and flowers and green trees.

As the days went on more people were sick. Would the food and water last until the ship came to land? Some of it would have to be kept for the sailors on the ship going back to England.

Two months went by. Everyone was tired. No one was very clean, for there was no fresh water to wash in.

At last one day a sailor called, "Land, ho!" What a hurrying and scurrying up on deck there was as the passengers all tried to see the shore! As the ship came near they could see evergreen trees growing near the water.

It was not warm Virginia, with its sunshine and flowers. It was Cape Cod, and it was winter. There were no friends to welcome the Pilgrims, no houses to live in. But they had come to land, and so they knelt and thanked God for bringing them safely to the new country.

They sailed a little farther and came into a sheltered harbor.

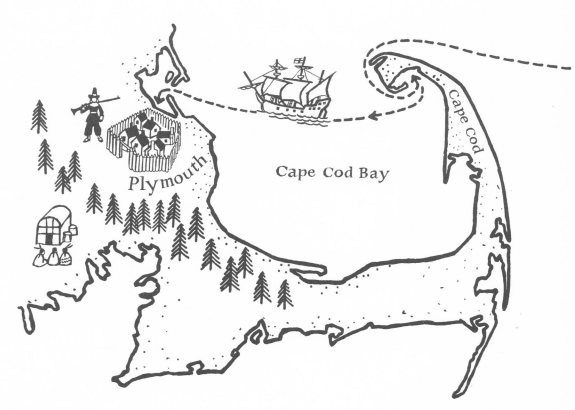

THE NEW LAND

Everyone would have liked to go on shore to walk on the good, firm ground. The women could hardly wait to wash all the dirty clothes. But first some of the men went to see if it was safe.

There would be Indians. The settlers had heard all kinds of stories about Indians. So the men carried their guns. They would not shoot except to protect themselves.

One of the men who went ashore was Myles Standish. He was a soldier and he had been training some of the men to use guns. Another was Stephen Hopkins, father of the Hopkins children.

On the *Mayflower,* Giles, Constance, and Damaris waited and waited for their father to come back. Oceanus slept and slept, as babies do.

The men waded through the ice-cold water, pulling the ship's boat up on the beach.

They walked along the shore and there seemed to be nothing but sand and sand and more sand. They cut some sweet-smelling branches of juniper, a kind of evergreen, and took them back to the ship. That night the settlers had a warm wood fire.

Some of the women and children on the *Mayflower* went ashore as soon as they could and had a wash day. There was a pond of fresh water near the beach. It was good to have clean, fresh clothes again.

The *Mayflower* had brought a small sailboat or fishing boat. This had to be taken ashore and mended. Some of the men worked on it.

Meanwhile other men went on looking for corn. They had heard about it from others who had been to this new land. They would trade with the Indians for seed to plant.

If they could not find corn, everyone might die of hunger. The seeds they had brought from England might not grow.

They looked everywhere. Once they saw some Indians and a dog, but these ran away into the woods.

They kept on looking.

No corn – but an old kettle half-buried in the sand. A ship's kettle – how did it come there?

No corn – but a pot hung over the place where a fire had been.

No corn – but small hills of sand. The men dug down into one and – there was a little old basket filled with corn! Now they had corn to plant. They found other baskets. These were big baskets, and it took two men to carry one. They filled their pockets with corn. Some day they would find the Indians and pay them for it.

One day they did see some more Indians. These Indians were not friendly. They shot at the settlers with their bows and arrows. The men shot back with their guns. After the Indians had gone, the settlers picked up many arrows on the sand.

Now the people on the *Mayflower* decided to sail across the bay and find a place to build their homes. They sent the fishing boat first to find a good harbor. Then the *Mayflower* sailed across to a place marked on the map. It was called Plymouth. The settlers called it New Plymouth because they had sailed from Plymouth in England.

It was a cold December day when some of the settlers landed. Once again they knelt and thanked God for His care of them.

This was a good place for homes. Indians had lived here, and there were fields where corn had been grown. There was rich black earth for planting and plenty of fresh water.

NEW HOMES
IN A NEW LAND

The winter was not a cold one, but it seemed long to the settlers. Many of them were sick. Many of them died. It was a sad time for everyone.

Some people stayed on the ship and others went ashore to work. They took with them some boards that they had brought on the ship. They also cut down trees and made rough boards. First they built a house to hold food—and some of the sick people stayed in this house. There were two smaller houses; one was used to keep supplies and one was for the sick people. One terrible night the thatched roof of the larger house caught fire. From the *Mayflower*, Giles, Constance, and Damaris could see the flames. The men on shore put out the fire.

With a great deal of hard work, the men built seven small houses. Now the Hopkins family had a home of their own.

And at last spring came.

There were new leaves on the trees and flowers in woods and fields. Birds sang in the trees. The country was no longer cold and wintry and bare; it was green and friendly and beautiful.

Almost everyone was weak and thin, for there had been so much sickness and not enough to eat. But weather for planting seeds was coming. Giles, Constance, and Damaris were happy to be out in the spring sunshine.

Ever since they had landed, the settlers had been finding new trees and plants in this new land. They also found many trees and flowers that they had known in England. They told each other about them as if they were meeting old friends. Here are oaks—and walnut and birch trees—ash and wild cherry and plum. And here are strawberries and watercress!

In April the *Mayflower* went back to England. Now the settlers were alone in the new country. Alone—except for the Indians.

Sometimes the settlers saw smoke from Indian fires. They saw Indians, too, but the Indians always ran away.

One day a tall Indian walked right into the village and spoke to the settlers in English. He had learned it from some of the sea captains who had come to that part of the country. His name was Samoset.

The people of Plymouth were surprised to see that the Indian wore so few clothes. It was still cold weather and how could he have only that little piece of leather around his waist? They gave him an old coat.

Later he brought another Indian named Squanto, who spoke better English, because he had been taken to England on a ship. The two told the Pilgrims why there were so few Indians in that part of the country. Many of them had died of a sickness.

It was fine to have a friendly Indian there in the daytime. But when night came the settlers wished he would go away. He stayed, so they let him sleep in the Hopkins' house but watched him all night.

Did Giles, Constance, and Damaris stay awake wondering about their strange visitor? We do not know.

After this, the Indian chief, Massasoit, came to visit.

The people of Plymouth made a place for the chief outside one of the houses they were building. They put boards and blankets on the ground and a green rug and cushions for Massasoit to sit on.

The Indians came to the meeting wearing leggings of deerskin. Their faces and bodies were painted in bright colors. The chief was painted dark red and he wore a necklace of white beads. The settlers went to the meeting in their best clothes, with a trumpet and drums. The Governor wore a red sash and a feather in his hat.

The settlers gave the Indian chief two shining knives and a copper chain to hang around his neck. Massasoit promised to be friendly. When his people came to Plymouth they would not bring bows and arrows with them. The promise of friendship was kept for fifty years.

Squanto, the friendly Indian, stayed in Plymouth. He showed the settlers how to plant corn in the Indian way. The Indians put small dead fish in each place where the seed was planted. This fertilized the corn and helped it to grow.

That year men, women, and children worked hard, planting. And that year there was a good crop of corn. Everyone worked to gather in the harvest.

A TIME
OF THANKSGIVING

The Pilgrims decided to have a special day to thank God for all He had given them. They had done this at harvest time in England.

Now they wanted to have a Thanksgiving feast and invite the Indian chief and his people.

And what a feast it was! Men went out into the woods to shoot deer and wild turkeys. The women cooked and baked. Only fifty-one settlers had lived through the winter—and half of them were children. Only a few women to do all the cooking! The older children helped as much as they could. By now Oceanus Hopkins was walking, and a new baby, Peregrine White, slept in his cradle. Peregrine was born on the *Mayflower* when it was anchored off Cape Cod. His name meant wanderer or pilgrim.

The day of the Thanksgiving dinner was warm and pleasant. Long tables were set out-of-doors. Probably the Pilgrims dressed in the best clothes they had, the men wearing their big, wide hats instead of work caps.

Then Massasoit, the great chief, came and the settlers must have counted the long, long line of Indians that followed him. One-two . . . twenty . . . forty . . . fifty . . . sixty . . . yes, there were ninety! Somehow there would be food for all.

And there was. Massasoit and his men had done their share, for they brought deer to the feast.

The Indian chief and the governor of Plymouth sat at one table. Some sat at tables—some on the ground. Elder Brewster, the minister, said a prayer, giving thanks to God for homes and food and safety in a new land.

The Indians may have understood about the prayer, for their people had a Thanksgiving prayer of their own. They gave thanks to their God, who made "the trees grow, the corn grow, and all kinds of fruits."

After the feast the settlers played games. The Indians danced. Myles Standish brought out his soldiers and they drilled as the Indians watched. The Indians stayed for three days.

The Pilgrims did not forget the hard times. They knew there would be difficult times to come. Still, they felt they had many things to be thankful for. They had food and houses and warm fires. The Indians were their friends. They were free in this new land. Free to work, to make their homes, to worship God in their own way.

Perhaps they sang the hymn they had brought to the New World with them:

"Praise God from whom all blessings flow,
Praise Him all creatures here below. . . ."

And if they did, Giles, Constance, and Damaris sang with them.